Mi Life

Miriam E. Lewis

Parson's Porch Books
www.parsonsporchbooks.com

Mi Life
ISBN: Softcover 978-1-951472-29-0
Copyright © 2019 by Miriam Lewis

All rights reserved. No part of this book may be reproduced or transmitted in any form or by any means, electronic or mechanical, including photocopying, recording, or by any information storage and retrieval system, without permission in writing from the publisher.

Mi Life

Contents

Introduction 7

Chapter One 9

Chapter Two 11

Chapter Three 16

Chapter Four 18

Chapter Five 21

Chapter Six 25

Chapter Seven 32

Introduction

Once within the everlasting arms of the Eternal God, the Lord said to my Lord, "Let us make a woman child. Through her life, she shall revive her ancestry and future generations to a familial deliverance."

Chapter One

On a summer afternoon at the Old Fort Campbell hospital in 1977, Sgt. Mercury L. Lewis and Cheryl Thomas Lewis welcomed a daughter, into the world. They named her Miriam Enochlyn Lewis. Her date of birth was literally 7-7-77. The blessed child was me. I shall tell you of an epic life wherein I have found as well as continue searching for depth and meaning.

Three days after my birth, Mom and I were discharged. My infant life was busy, full of trips to Southern states where the Lewis family was to relocate to one at a time, all within a time period of ten years.

I recall one road-trip where Dad was asking my older sister Shelbi and me about the street signs. "What does that sign say, Shelbi?"

"Stop," Shelbi responded confidently. Shelbi got about five more sign questions correct. I started to discern that Shelbi, four-and-a-half years old, was gifted.

About a year later, Shelbi was reviewing the Little Golden Book, "The Little Red Hen" with me. That's right, some mysterious way, I had learned to read, and I was excellent at reading Old Maid cards and Little Golden Books.

The next year my favorite teacher, Shelbi, reluctantly taught me how to write. Then on the first day of school, she taught me how to count as we waited in the cafetorium for our teachers to come in and take us to our assigned classes.

Thus, was the first miracle of childhood: reading, writing, and arithmetic primarily mastered as a toddler. Before school began.

Chapter Two

There was only half a day of school in Head start. So at noon, Mom brought me back to our fabulous home. It was a row house duplex. The inside of our home was finely furnished with soft golden chairs, a floral sofa and tables with doors that opened and closed to reveal a collection of records. The collection was from Gospel to soft rock to jazz. There were greats like Sara Jordan Powell, Edwin Hawkins, Barry Manilow, and Ella Fitzgerald in those end table cabinets. All this was in the living room along with a large color T.V. I remember so many movies like Mahogany, The Wizard of Oz and The Wiz. Sometimes we watched The Muppet Show or Hee-Haw. Nonetheless, my favorite prime time show was The Carol Burnett Show.

There was an upstairs with four bedrooms. My Uncle Terry (14 years old), Shelbi and me, and my now two baby sisters bunked up there. Of course my parents did too. But let's talk more about this Terry guy. The younger brother of my mom, he lived with us and attended school in D.C. at Glen Haven High. He, early in life, had accepted his calling as a comedian and practical joker. But for now he was just our male nanny. If there was ever a word for this, I would pick, "Manny". However, his being black, it sounds too close to the racial slur, "Mammy".

Sundays were the greatest. I don't know what the preacher was ever saying, but the choir was a hit! Min. Harvey Lewis, Jr. directed the choir with his whole body. It was like watching a spirit-filled band drum major direct a gospel choir. He'd also written many of the songs and they were national hits. Well, at least to us children of the parents who toured with him. The choir was getting engagements from Constitution Hall to Carnegie Hall. The photos on those album covers kept in me in awe as I marveled at the titles like "He's the Greatest!" and "Happy as a Tree". One picture caught Lewis directing in what seemed to be mid-air.

He and his family were invited to our house for dinner several times. Usually, a crab or lobster feast. He had a beautiful wife, Gwen, and two toddler children. The kids were Ellaina, age 6, and Vernon, age 3.

After church, we'd go out to eat with preacher friends from church and their families at Chesapeake Bay Restaurant in Maryland. We church members got a private room complete with booster seats for the little children. One of my earliest memories is the fried shrimp somebody ordered for me being thrown into my mouth by my little fingers accompanied by french fries and cole slaw with hush puppies. I was allowed to drink a whole 16 ounce glass of soda at the age of three. I never wet the bed.

Then came the bad news: Director Lewis died. It was pneumonia. I didn't know what "die" meant. But our household had to go back to Memphis because Muddear died to. Then Dad finished his training in Texas, New York, and Washington, D.C. We immediately relocated to Memphis for the family and the help. Dad was now stationed in Korea. He would come to visit us as the army allowed. Now, I was in kindergarten. Mom got us carpools and house pools (Gram kept Shelbi and me most of the time while Mom kept the babies, Oshea and Natalie.) These times were hard on everyone named above that was living. Sometimes my ten-year-old aunt would keep us in the daytime when there was no one else to hire. Along with three other cousins and the soap operas on, this got wild. To sum up, what was watched on General Hospital, wound up playing a role in my sisters' and my life that led us to the General Mental Hospital. No further discussion.

By first grade, Dad moved us back with him to Fort Campbell, Kentucky. The sensuality slowed down. Happy days were back. But there was another demon to conquer: offensive violence.

Chapter Three

We moved into another row house in Ft. Campbell, but this time we lived in the single occupancy. There was no adjoining home to ours on the building. Shelbi and I went to school with a diversity of races of children. We listened to pop music now. The German kids taught us how to swear in German and Chinese. We also learned how to count to ten and play hand games in German language. I also learned to sign the alphabet in sign language.

For additional cultivation of skills, Mom enrolled Shelbi and me in piano lessons at Mrs. Johnson's house. In about four months, I was playing with two hands. Shelbi no longer showed interest in piano by this time.

One morning, as I rose, I felt that God had given me supernatural power to protect myself from harm. I told Shelbi. She tested my awareness by running towards me in curiosity and I threw her over my back. She replied, "That was cool!" So we practiced fighting that morning. But that innocent play was about to change.

Shelbi started getting into fights at school. Usually, I stood by as a witness. Sometimes, I fought others based upon her recruitment. I even went to the office to hear the verdict of the menaces that fought when I did not fight. One day, the principal cleared the office of all the children who really did not fight. When I went back to the classroom the teacher and the children encouraged me not to fight again because I was so talented. They prophesied, "You are not going to be like your sister."

From this day forward, I tried to stay out of Shelbi's personal blues.

Chapter Four

Dad was medically discharged from the military and after a long wait for a severance check, the Lewis family began civilian life. The throes of our settling down had been rough.

For example, we lived at a church couple's home in their basement. Mom sowed a thousand-dollar seed to Tilton Ministries to release our finances. She did this because she felt Satan was hindering our progress. The seed-sowing worked. After the money came from the government, Dad bought a ranch style house in the Green Acres suburb of Clarksville, TN. We had a green lawn and backyard. Dad planted a flower garden out front near the pine trees. We had bought a puppy while living in Fort Campbell, named Golden and we brought him with us. Dad built his doghouse in the backyard. These were the best years of our lives.

My sisters and I developed musical talents and etiquette here through 4-H club and home tea parties. By the time I was ten years old, I led my sisters, Oshea and Natalie in high tea wherein we all had a part in cooking pastries and setting the table at 12 noon at least three times a week.

Shelbi would be in charge. She oversaw the cleaning and concerts we had after cleaning that were just for the four of us. Our favorite artists were now Milton Bronson and the Thompson Community Choir. We would start a rock group and sing to the ripping guitar of "Everything Moves by the Power of God". We snuck pop music on by Phil Collins and Michael Jackson because my parents were gone all day in the summertime. My parents had culture but did not allow "worldly entertainment". No pop or R & B music. No watching movies or T.V. shows that were violent, raunchy, or contained adult language.

Believe it or not, we all stayed out of trouble for the most part. Sometimes, there was some rebellion when school started due to peer pressure. We got grounded for smoking. (Shelbi and me). But I quit cold turkey by the sixth grade.

By then, Mom and Dad's finances took a turn for the worst and the family was relocated to Memphis, Tennessee.

Chapter Five

Dad, Mom, kids, and dog all were packed up in a white Chevy van for the long haul down to Memphis. I remember the U2 song playing in my teary-eyed and weary head, "I Still Haven't Found What I'm Looking For". Once, again I was being uprooted from my friends and church family. Only this time I met a new enemy: poverty. If ever there was time to be a soldier it was now.

We moved in with my Dad's parents in the country. Now we lived in a different idea of "Green Acres". More like Ava Gabor leaving city life and going with her husband to the countryside in the old sitcom. This was not the wealthy green pasture of Clarksville. This was our post Jim Crow South version of the Color Purple. Not in reference to the serious topic matter in the book, mind you. Only in allusion to the shanties and barrenness of the place.

My grandfather had bought the property outright to own and farm from an Italian man. Granddaddy Enos, as we called our father's dad was a military veteran. He was extremely practical and had achieved only a ninth-grade education before he married Grandma Mary and started his family. They had ten children. Perfectly divided into five boys and five girls. Two of the women died as young adults. Now, there were eight children left to hold the legacy down.

Arrangements for our family board were as follows: Shelbi on the couch in the living room. Mom and Dad in the guest bedroom. Oshea, Natalie, and I in the other guest bedroom. Grandma, gave each of us sisters some clean mu-mus to sleep in. The floor was so dusty, house shoes were a must.

I had a lot of clothes, but not enough shoes. Dad kept rubber gluing my white canvas shoes' soles to the canvas tops for months. There were holes in them, and they soon began to appear dirty. One of my sisters wet the bed and soiled the rest of us. However, grandma would never let us take a soaking bath. We could only wash up at the sink. She insisted that she was "saving the water". I don't recall many hairdos professionally. The kids at school were appalled by my grungy look and teased me proclaiming that I smelled, was tacky and was poor. But help was on the way.

There was a school spelling bee that Grandma let me bathe for and participate in. I studied many days in preparation for it. Then, I won it.

The winner was responsible for representing the school at other spelling bees throughout the district, so I was permitted to take a bath more often. I wore church clothes to the district spelling bees. Later, I received a new pair of shoes from the science teacher.

Moreover, I was discovered as a poet and prose writer. I won an award at the close of the year for excellence in poetry. The quality of my education proved to be a poverty crusher. God was blessing my obedience and dutifulness.

Chapter Six

After hygienic and academic triumph in the sixth grade, I was promoted to the seventh grade. I started the seventh grade at Manassas Junior High. Our family moved in from Dad's business building downtown on Main Street to Gram's house in North Memphis. I was glad to be back in the city. The experience I had sixth grade year with overcoming poverty through hard work and faith in God empowered me with confidence to tackle the academic world with award-winning spirit. I won music as well as scholastic trophies and was often asked to sing solos at award banquets and Christmas concerts.

By the end of the seventh grade I ranked number one in overall grade point average in my seventh-grade class. I had repeat success in eighth grade. However, due to academic boredom and bullying by a sophomore, I transferred to Snowden Junior High. This was one of the city's college preparatory schools.

At Snowden, fighting was discouraged completely. The school was large, but cozy. The students were mannerable and I quickly made friends. Pity parties and low self-esteem were not esteemed at all. I throve under the auspice of an expansive community of friends, teachers, and good parenting.

I won Soprano of the year in choir and many additional scholastic honors including science and English. I was recommended for the STEM program (Back then we called it math-sciences.) at Central. Yet, I opted for the more relaxing music program since I had already been assigned to Overton after a very successful audition.

At Overton High school, I learned what it really meant to be a musician. Hard work, cooperation and ethics were the top lessons.

Then creativity and booster club fundraisers for income. I was doted on by the choirmaster, Mrs. Hedgeman as well as the school principal, Mr. White. I learned to take care of myself above all else and to have a healthy ego.

Howbeit, when the mentors in my life tried to break my spirit, I was empowered enough to stop the mental attack. For example, the choir was about to go on an expensive trip to Canada to participate in a festival. I wanted to fund-raise my entire trip as I had done before at Snowden. I counted up the cost. The trip cost $960. I would need 32 boxes of $1.00 candy. There were 30 bars in each box. That was all the money I needed-$960.00. Reluctantly, the teacher let me check all that candy out. As she feared, I could not sell it all. Overwhelmed, by peer jesting due to the candy fiasco, Caucasian hellcats terrorizing me over my perfect appearance, and a newborn niece at home (Shelbi's daughter, Navia), I felt led to leave and return to STEM for some stability in life. At Overton, somehow, I was encouraged to believe in myself with no boundaries. However, that year, junior year, I found the limits.

After a lot of singing (moaning, rather), "Hand on the Plow", and praying in the Spirit, I got my transfer to Central. The students welcomed me with love. I finished out the semester in rehab. My parents now were experiencing wonderful jobs. They could afford tremendous health care for the family. I was finally placed in the psychiatric care of African American professionals. Care that I depended on for most of my life.

I was placed in group therapy in twelfth grade. This helped me survive senior year. My prom was a blast. I graduated with a 3.69 GPA and accepted to five Negro Colleges' electrical engineering programs. Nonetheless, due to financial and mental hardships, I stayed home and tried to commute to the University of Memphis.

With no driver's license, I was confined to the bus stops of Memphis. Literally "walking with my feet ten feet off of Beale", I took a few classes at Shelby State Community College's main campus. It is on Union near Beale Street. A big buff guy friend of Natalie's escorted me downtown to shop many afternoons after school so I would not walk alone. But things were about to change for the better.

Let's backtrack for precision. My family had moved to South Memphis in the winter of 1995. The house was much larger, as we bottom three sisters were now becoming more independent and needed growing room. Shelbi found an East Memphis apartment for her and Navia. She was still unmarried.

After my high school graduation, Mom finished a Theology degree from Jacksonville

Theological Seminary. Dad was in the second year of his COGIC church, The Way of Truth Deliverance Church of God in Christ. I was in school making as in engineering and failing everything else. The other two siblings were working and going to high school. We were moving forward. The only problem we had was that ghetto environment we lived in. Nonetheless, we, as a family, strove to make a difference. As years advanced, I got a trade in clerical specialty. This was the preface to my receiving white-collar jobs. The ghetto clique from the former neighborhood followed us here. The lies they told me along with our family rivals' seducing me out of my income kept putting holes in my pocket. After an outburst at dinner, Mom and Dad called the police on me. I was escorted without being mirandized to Memphis Mental Health Institute on Poplar and Dunlap. When the staff found out about the girl gang, they told me to stay away from them for the sake of my mental health. I heeded this advice and was discharged. After six months of keeping my nose clean, we moved to the middle class.

Goodbye, hoodlums! Hello, Hickory Hill Community!

Chapter Seven

While my family lived in Hickory Hill, a boy at University of Memphis tried to discourage my spirit by calling the community Hickory Hood. But it was an affluent place with a large mall, a Barnes and Noble Bookseller, and a Red Lobster.

I was able to reconnect with my African roots as I made Nigerian and many other diversities of friends from African nations. I ate African cuisine, was given African clothes to wear, and was taught widely spoken African languages. My interpersonal skills improved, and I was respected as a fledgling minister instead of being harassed for being a good person as the kids teased me for at Overton.

I was no longer scammed by cons. I was hired at three different jobs consecutively at three jobs on Winchester Road.

I worked some white collar in the medical field in between fast food jobs. The medical jobs did not last long because the companies' management noticed signs of my easily being influenced by negative peers. Reliable transportation was a problem as well. Yet, while working at Popeye's Chicken, I aced Driver's Ed. When I went back to the DMV, I passed the written part of the test. I had no vehicle to take the road test. I had to come back later to finish the process.

As a turn for the better, Natalie and Oshea moved out, leaving me the last dependent of my parents.

Mom's birthday gift from Dad was a suburban three level home in prestigious Walls, Mississippi. It was a villa built on a lake in a subdivision called Grandview Lake. The street we lived on was Grandview Cove. The next year I was 29 years old. I received my driver's license. Three months later, I got a Mercedes Benz for my birthday.

It was presented on Father's Day in advance of my actual birthday.

However, God instructed me to sell it to my father in exchange of the arrears I owed him since Hickory Hill. God was preparing me to move out debt-free. The disability I incurred in the eleventh grade, left my parents thinking that I was using my illness as a "crutch"

and not trying to do my part. So selling the gift was step one to gaining freedom from this allegation. Gram gave me a car to replace it. She put her name on the title to keep it from being stolen from me. When I felt confident enough not to be swindled, I bought the title for myself. My judgment was great. I drove that car 'til it couldn't take it anymore. I passed a semester of Calculus and Music Theory. Two very hard mathematical classes. (Music Theory has a lot of intricate counting.) I attended parties. I ran errands. I attended plays and concerts. I drove myself to my church's Christmas Gala.

My pastor announced to the church when the grades came in that I made a B in the Calculus. Everything was looking up.

I moved out of the house twice before Dad sold the Grandview estate cash for key. Mom and Dad and I lived in a temporary house with a mouse in it. Then we packed up and went to Aunt Lisa's in the exurbs. I put in an application for John Madison Exum Towers, a high rise for independent living. The residents included senior citizens and the disabled. I got the key in November 2011. Nine months later, my parents moved in with me. My Dad was moving his belongings in what Dad dubbed his exposed homelessness an "open-air thrift store. Beforehand, he was sleeping in the street to keep watch on his merchandise. God had protected him from street harm as well as the Great Flood of 2010. My dad is a survivor. His military training came in handy that year he was out there. His spiritual warfare did too.

When Dad turned 62, my apartment complex, JMET, found my parents an apartment on the East side of the building on the third floor. They moved in immediately. The apartments go like hotcakes because the rates are also affordable.

The conclusion of the matter is I have been living here at this apartment six years. I have stability. I am under doctor's care. I have forgiven everyone. Parents, siblings, enemies and classmates. However, I have learned to be more cautious of who I associate with. My parents live in a luxury two-bedroom retirement living facility around friends and family all with their own apartments. I love to visit my parents there. It is beautiful there any time of year.

Oshea has two sons, Joshua and Morgan, who reside with her in Texas. Natalie is married with two sons and works at home and in her church. Shelbi married and has two more children. A daughter, Zoe and a son, Neko. Navia is a successful businesswoman, climbing the corporate ladder at Federal Express. She is also a Tennessee state board certified cosmetologist.

The moral of the story is this: living faithful to God pays off. People might tease you when you are well-bred, but I would rather have running water and a pest-free home than fit in with haters that would destroy me if they had the chance.

My haters are many, my lovers are few, but God is for me. I am paying off debts in order to finish my last 37 hours in electrical engineering after much failure, struggle and discouragement. However, my testimony has always been: "Help is on the way!"

After I suffer enough, He will come through to a desirable outcome.

God has helped me every time. God will help me. He will help M.E.! My name is Miriam E. Lewis. Abbreviated, it is Miriam E.

My folks call me Mimi. I have shortened Mimi to Mi. The story you have just read is Mi history. In essence, it is "Mi Life". I hope this has blessed you.

www.ingramcontent.com/pod-product-compliance
Lightning Source LLC
Chambersburg PA
CBHW052128110526
44592CB00013B/1797